MANAGED TO GET IT DONE
Your People Are a Reflection of You

J. Jerrell Bass

Table of Contents

Introduction

Management blends art and science, requiring empathy, strategy, and vision. This book aims to help you navigate this journey with seven key principles from top management experts. These principles offer practical strategies to improve your management skills and boost your team's performance.

Everyone has unique strengths, and understanding these can lead to long-term success. By aligning roles with individual talents, managers can unlock their team's full potential.

Trust is the foundation of effective management. It is emphasized that trust is built through consistency, integrity, and genuine care for team members. When managers foster a culture of trust, they inspire their teams to exceed expectations and achieve great results.

Continuous learning and professional growth are vital for both individual and organizational success. Prioritizing personal development boosts morale and productivity, ensuring team members are equipped for future challenges.

Insights from experts offer a comprehensive guide to effective management. Integrating these strategies can help you build a resilient, motivated, and high-performing team.

Great managers aren't born; they're made through dedication, experience, and a genuine desire to bring out the best in their people. This book provides you with the tools, insights, and strategies to become the leader your team needs. Use these principles to inspire, empower, and achieve exceptional results.

Chapter 1
Maximizing Human Potential

Introduction to the Importance of Human Potential

Imagine a world where every individual reaches their full potential, not just for personal success but for the betterment of society. This vision is not merely a utopian dream but a tangible goal that can be achieved through strategic and intentional management practices. As Jim Clifton and Jim Harter, authors with a deep understanding of organizational dynamics, we believe that maximizing human potential is critical for any organization aiming for success. This chapter delves into the profound impact that unlocking human potential can have on both individuals and organizations.

The Role of Managers

Managers play a pivotal role in this process. They are the catalysts that can transform a group of individuals into a high-performing team. Effective managers understand that their primary responsibility is not just to oversee tasks but to nurture the growth and development of their team members. By doing so, they create an environment where employees are motivated, engaged, and committed to achieving both personal and organizational goals.

Practical Strategies

Unlocking human potential requires a strategic approach that encompasses various aspects of management. Here are some practical strategies that managers can implement to foster an environment conducive to growth and development:

1.   Identify Strengths and Talents:
The first step in maximizing human potential is recognizing each team member's unique strengths and talents. CliftonStrengths, a widely used assessment tool, helps managers identify and leverage these strengths effectively. Managers can enhance productivity and job satisfaction by focusing on what employees do best.

2.   Set Expectations:
Clear and achievable goals give employees a sense of direction and purpose. Managers should work with their team members to set realistic expectations and create a roadmap for achieving them. This collaborative approach ensures everyone is on the same page and committed to the same objectives.

3.   Provide Continuous Feedback:
Regular feedback is essential for personal and professional growth. Managers should create a culture of continuous feedback, where constructive criticism and praise are given frequently. This helps employees understand their progress, identify areas for improvement, and stay motivated.

4.   Encourage Development Opportunities:
Investing in employee development is a win-win for the organization and its employees. Managers should encourage

team members to pursue training, certifications, and other learning opportunities aligned with their career goals. This enhances their skills and demonstrates the organization's commitment to their growth.

5.   Foster a Positive Work Environment:
A positive work environment is crucial for employee well-being and productivity. Managers should strive to create a culture of respect, inclusivity, and collaboration. This includes addressing conflicts promptly, recognizing achievements, and promoting a healthy work-life balance.

Case Study: Maximizing Potential in Action

Consider the example of a leading tech company that successfully implemented these strategies. The company's management team conducted strength assessments for all employees and realigned roles based on individual talents. They introduced a robust feedback system and provided extensive development opportunities, including mentorship programs and workshops. As a result, employee engagement and productivity soared, and the company experienced unprecedented growth.

The Broader Impact
Maximizing human potential has far-reaching implications beyond individual organizations. People who are empowered to reach their full potential contribute more effectively to their communities and society. This ripple effect can increase innovation, economic growth, and overall well-being.

Conclusion

Maximizing human potential is not a one-time effort but an ongoing process that requires commitment and dedication from managers and leaders. By implementing the strategies outlined in this chapter, managers can create an environment where employees thrive, leading to more tremendous success for individuals and organizations. As we continue to explore the principles of effective management, it is essential to remember that the accurate measure of a manager's success lies in their ability to unlock the potential within their team.

Detailed Breakdown of Strategies

To provide further insight into the practical application of these strategies, let us delve deeper into each one:

1.   Identify Strengths and Talents

Assessment Tools: Utilize tools like CliftonStrengths to identify individual strengths.

Strengths-Based Assignments: Align tasks and projects with employees' strengths to maximize efficiency and job satisfaction.

Strengths Conversations: Regularly discuss strengths and how they can be leveraged daily.

2.   Set Clear Expectations

Goal Setting: Use SMART goals (Specific, Measurable, Achievable, Relevant, Time-bound) to provide clear direction.

Role Clarity: Ensure each team member understands their role and responsibilities.

Performance Metrics: Develop metrics to measure progress and success.

3. Provide Continuous Feedback

Feedback Loops: Establish regular check-ins and performance reviews.

Constructive Criticism: Focus on specific behaviors and provide actionable advice for improvement.

Recognition and Praise: Acknowledge achievements and contributions to boost morale.

4. Encourage Development Opportunities

Training Programs: Offer access to training programs and workshops.

Career Pathing: Help employees map their career paths within the organization.

Mentorship: Pair employees with mentors to guide their development.

5. Foster a Positive Work Environment

Inclusivity: Promote diversity and inclusivity in the workplace.

Work-Life Balance: Encourage flexible work arrangements and respect for personal time.

Conflict Resolution: Address conflicts promptly and fairly to maintain a harmonious work environment.

Case Study: Tech Company Success Story

The management team's commitment to maximizing human potential at the tech company led to significant positive outcomes. Employees reported higher job satisfaction and engagement levels, and the company's innovative capabilities improved. The company also saw reduced turnover rates, as employees felt valued and invested in their roles.

The Role of Leadership

Leadership plays a crucial role in the successful implementation of these strategies. Leaders must lead by example, demonstrating a commitment to personal growth and development. They should also foster trust and open communication, where employees feel safe expressing their ideas and concerns.

Conclusion

Maximizing human potential is a journey that requires continuous effort and dedication. By adopting the strategies discussed in this chapter, managers can create a thriving work environment that benefits employees and the organization. As we progress in this book, we will explore additional principles and practices contributing to effective management and organizational success.

This concludes the first chapter of "Managed (To Get It Done)." The following chapters will build upon these foundational strategies, providing further insights and practical advice for managers seeking to enhance their leadership skills and drive organizational success.

Chapter 2
Building Trust and Motivating Beyond Authority

Introduction: The Essence of Trust and Motivation

In management, trust is the cornerstone of all successful relationships. Without trust, teams flounder, communication breaks down, and motivation wanes. This chapter, inspired by principles from "The Harvard Business Review Manager's Handbook," delves into the strategies for building trust and motivating employees beyond the boundaries of formal authority. We will explore practical techniques, real-world examples, and actionable insights to help managers create a trustworthy and highly motivated workforce.

The Foundations of Trust

Trust is an elusive yet essential element in any organization. It is built on transparency, consistency, and integrity. Managers who wish to foster trust must lead by example, demonstrating honesty and reliability in all their actions.

1.   Transparency and Open Communication

Open Door Policy: Encourage an environment where employees feel comfortable sharing their thoughts and concerns. An open-door policy promotes transparency and reduces the fear of speaking up.

Regular Updates: Keep team members informed about organizational changes, decisions, and strategies. Regular updates via meetings, emails, or newsletters help build a culture of openness.

Active Listening: Practice active listening by giving full attention to the speaker, acknowledging their points, and responding thoughtfully. This shows respect and builds trust.

2.   Consistency and Fairness
Consistent Actions: Align words with actions. Consistency in decision-making and behavior builds credibility.

Fair Treatment: Ensure fair treatment of all employees. Avoid favoritism and address issues of inequality promptly and fairly.

3.   Integrity and Accountability
Admit Mistakes: Acknowledge and learn from mistakes. Admitting errors openly fosters a culture of honesty.

Hold Everyone Accountable: Apply the same accountability standards to yourself as you do to your team. This demonstrates integrity and reinforces trust.

Motivating Beyond Authority
Motivation extends beyond the confines of formal authority. Effective managers inspire their teams through empowerment, recognition, and alignment of personal and organizational goals.

1. Empowerment through Delegation

Delegate Meaningfully: Assign tasks that challenge and utilize team members' strengths. Delegation shows trust in their abilities and promotes professional growth.

Provide Autonomy: Give employees the freedom to approach tasks in their way. Autonomy fosters creativity and ownership.

2. Recognition and Appreciation

Timely Recognition: Recognize achievements and contributions promptly. Timely appreciation boosts morale and motivation.

Public and Private Praise: Offer both public recognition and private appreciation. Public praise motivates the individual and inspires peers, while private praise feels more personal and sincere.

3. Aligning Goals

Personal Development Plans: Work with employees to create personal development plans that align with their career aspirations and the organization's objectives. This alignment ensures that individual efforts contribute to broader goals.

Meaningful Work: Assign tasks that have clear significance and impact. When employees see the value in their work, they are more motivated to excel.

Case Study: A Trust-Building Success Story

Consider the example of a mid-sized marketing firm that successfully built trust and motivated its employees beyond formal authority. The firm's management implemented transparency initiatives, including monthly town hall meetings where leaders shared updates and answered questions openly. They also established a system for recognizing contributions, where employees could nominate peers for awards.

One notable instance involved a project that went awry due to a managerial oversight. The manager admitted the mistake in a team meeting, discussed lessons learned, and outlined steps to prevent future occurrences. This honesty and accountability strengthened the team's trust in leadership.

Additionally, the firm empowered its employees by delegating significant responsibilities and providing the autonomy to execute tasks creatively. This approach led to innovative campaigns that garnered industry awards and boosted employee morale.

The Broader Implications of Trust and Motivation

Building trust and motivating employees has far-reaching implications. Trust reduces friction in communication and collaboration, leading to higher efficiency and better outcomes. Motivated employees are more engaged, productive, and committed to the organization's success.

Research shows that high-trust organizations outperform their counterparts in key metrics, including employee retention, customer satisfaction, and financial performance. Trust and motivation are not merely "nice-to-have" qualities but critical drivers of organizational success.

Practical Applications: Tools and Techniques

To translate these principles into practice, here are some tools and techniques managers can use:

1. Feedback Mechanisms: Implement regular feedback mechanisms, such as one-on-one meetings and anonymous surveys, to gauge employee sentiments and areas for improvement.
2. Recognition Programs: Develop structured recognition programs that celebrate achievements, big and small.
3. Development Opportunities: Offer continuous learning and development opportunities, such as workshops, courses, and mentorship programs.
4. Transparent Communication Channels: Use communication platforms to allow open dialogue and information sharing.

Conclusion

Building trust and motivating employees beyond formal authority requires a multifaceted approach rooted in transparency, consistency, integrity, empowerment, and recognition. By fostering a culture of trust and motivation, managers can unlock the full potential of their teams, driving both individual and organizational success.

As we continue our exploration of effective management practices in the subsequent chapters, remember that the principles of trust and motivation form the foundation upon which all other strategies are built. Mastering these elements will set the stage for a thriving, high-performing organization.

This concludes the second chapter of "Managed (To Get It Done)." The following chapters will build on these foundational concepts, providing deeper insights and practical guidance for managers striving to create a dynamic and successful work environment.

Chapter 3
Investing in Personal Development

Introduction: The Lifeblood of Organizational Growth

In an ever-evolving business landscape, the key to sustained organizational success lies in the continuous personal development of its employees. This chapter, inspired by Scott Jeffrey Miller, Todd Davis, and Victoria Roos Olsson, delves into the importance of investing in personal development and provides practical strategies to integrate this crucial practice into your management approach. By fostering an environment where personal growth is prioritized, managers can unlock the full potential of their teams, leading to enhanced performance, innovation, and job satisfaction.

The Importance of Personal Development

Personal development is self-improvement through activities that enhance skills, knowledge, and well-being. It is an investment that yields significant returns for both individuals and organizations.

1.   Enhancing Skills and Competencies

Continuous Learning: Encourage a culture of continuous learning where employees are motivated to acquire new skills and knowledge. This can be achieved through training programs, workshops, and online courses.

Skill Diversification: Promote the development of a diverse skill set. Employees who are versatile and adaptable are more valuable to the organization.

2.   Boosting Employee Morale and Engagement

Career Advancement: Personal development initiatives signal employees that the organization is invested in their future. This boosts morale and increases engagement.

Job Satisfaction: Employees with opportunities for growth and development are generally more satisfied with their jobs, leading to lower turnover rates.

3.   Driving Innovation and Creativity

Innovative Thinking: A commitment to personal development fosters a mindset of continuous improvement and innovation. Employees are more likely to think creatively and propose new ideas.

Adaptability to Change: In a rapidly changing business environment, continuously developing employees are better equipped to adapt to new challenges and opportunities.

Strategies for Investing in Personal Development

Effective personal development requires a strategic approach that aligns with individual aspirations and organizational goals.

1.   Creating a Personal Development Plan (PDP)

Individual Assessments: Conduct individual assessments to identify strengths, weaknesses, and areas for development.

Use tools such as self-assessments, peer reviews, and performance evaluations.

Goal Setting: Work with employees to set SMART (Specific, Measurable, Achievable, Relevant, Time-bound) goals for their development. These goals should align with both personal aspirations and organizational needs.

Regular Reviews: Schedule regular reviews to track progress, provide feedback, and adjust goals as necessary.

2. Providing Learning and Development Opportunities

Training Programs: Offer various training programs, including technical skills, leadership development, and soft skills training. Tailor these programs to meet the specific needs of your team.

Mentorship and Coaching: Establish mentorship and coaching programs where experienced employees can guide and support the development of their peers.

Tuition Reimbursement: Provide financial support for employees seeking further education or professional certifications.

3. Fostering a Learning Culture

Encourage Curiosity: Promote a culture that values curiosity and a growth mindset. Encourage employees to explore new areas of interest and take on challenging projects.

Knowledge Sharing: Create knowledge-sharing platforms, such as internal workshops, seminars, and online forums. Encourage employees to share their expertise and learn from each other.

4. Leveraging Technology for Development

E-Learning Platforms: Utilize e-learning platforms that offer a wide range of courses and resources. These platforms provide flexibility for employees to learn at their own pace.

Virtual Workshops: Organize virtual workshops and webinars to provide access to expert knowledge and industry trends.

Performance Tracking Tools: Implement tools that track and analyze performance data to identify development needs and measure the impact of training programs.

Case Study: A Personal Development Success Story

Consider the example of a technology company that successfully integrated personal development into its organizational strategy. The company implemented a comprehensive personal development program that included individual assessments, goal setting, and a variety of learning opportunities.

One notable initiative was establishing a mentorship program where senior engineers mentored junior employees. This program enhanced technical skills and fostered strong relationships and a collaborative culture. Additionally, the company offered tuition reimbursement for employees pursuing further education, resulting in a highly skilled and motivated workforce.

As a result, the company experienced significant improvements in employee satisfaction, retention rates, and overall performance. The continuous investment in personal development also led to a culture of innovation, with employees regularly proposing and implementing new ideas that drove business growth.

The Broader Implications of Personal Development

Investing in personal development has far-reaching implications for both individuals and organizations. It leads to a more skilled, motivated, and adaptable workforce better equipped to meet the challenges of a dynamic business environment.

Organizations prioritizing personal development are considered employers of choice, attracting top talent and retaining high-performing employees. This commitment to growth and development also enhances the organization's reputation and competitiveness in the market.

Practical Applications: Tools and Techniques

To translate these principles into practice, here are some tools and techniques managers can use:

1.   Development Plans: Create and implement personal development plans for each employee, outlining their goals, learning opportunities, and progress milestones.
2.   Training and Workshops: Offer regular training sessions and workshops on relevant topics, both in-person and online.
3.   Mentorship Programs: Establish structured mentorship programs that pair experienced employees with those seeking guidance and development.
4.   Learning Management Systems (LMS): Utilize LMS platforms to provide access to a wide range of courses and track employee progress.

5.   Feedback Mechanisms: Implement regular feedback mechanisms, such as performance reviews and one-on-one meetings, to discuss development needs and achievements.

Conclusion

Personal development is a strategic priority that drives individual and organizational success. By fostering a culture of continuous learning and growth, managers can unlock the full potential of their teams, leading to enhanced performance, innovation, and job satisfaction.

As we continue our exploration of effective management practices in the subsequent chapters, remember that personal development is not a one-time effort but an ongoing journey. Embrace the principles and strategies this chapter discusses to create a dynamic and thriving organization.

This concludes the third chapter of "Managed (To Get It Done)." The following chapters will build on these foundational concepts, providing deeper insights and practical guidance for managers striving to create a dynamic and successful work environment.

Chapter 4
The Power of Asking the Right Questions

Introduction: Unleashing Potential Through Inquiry

Effective leadership often hinges on the ability to ask the right questions. In his work on leadership and development, Ryan Hawk emphasizes that powerful questions can unlock hidden potential, foster innovation, and drive meaningful conversations. This chapter will explore the art of asking the right questions and how this skill can transform management practices. By delving into the techniques and strategies for effective questioning, managers can enhance their ability to lead, inspire, and achieve outstanding results.

The Essence of Powerful Questions

1.   Defining Powerful Questions

Open-Ended Nature: Powerful questions are typically open-ended, encouraging expansive thinking and detailed responses. They begin with words like "how," "why," "what," and "can you explain."

Purpose-Driven: These questions are designed with a clear purpose in mind, whether it's to gain deeper insights, challenge assumptions, or inspire creativity.

2.   The Impact of Effective Questioning

Encouraging Reflection: Asking thought-provoking questions prompts individuals to reflect on their experiences, beliefs, and actions, leading to greater self-awareness and personal growth.

Driving Engagement: Questions stimulating discussion and debate foster a more engaged and collaborative team environment.

Facilitating Problem-Solving: Managers can guide their teams toward innovative solutions by framing questions that encourage analytical thinking.

Techniques for Asking the Right Questions
1.   The Art of Framing

Clarity and Precision: Ensure your questions are clear and concise. Avoid ambiguity to prevent misunderstandings.

Contextual Relevance: Tailor your questions to the specific context and audience. Consider the unique perspectives and experiences of your team members.

2.   Listening Actively

Full Attention: Active listening involves giving your full attention to the speaker, demonstrating genuine interest, and avoiding interruptions.

Reflective Responses: Reflect on what you have heard to confirm understanding and encourage further elaboration.

3.   Encouraging Depth

Follow-Up Questions: Use follow-up questions to delve deeper into the initial response. This can uncover underlying issues or opportunities for growth.

Challenging Assumptions: Ask questions that challenge assumptions and encourage critical thinking. This can lead to new insights and perspectives.

Practical Applications: Scenarios and Examples

1. Performance Reviews

Exploratory Questions: Instead of asking, "Did you meet your targets?" try "What strategies did you find most effective in meeting your targets, and why?"

Development Focus: Ask questions about future growth, such as "What skills do you want to develop over the next quarter?"

2. Team Meetings

Idea Generation: In brainstorming sessions, ask, "What unconventional approaches can we take to solve this problem?"

Feedback Solicitation: Encourage feedback with questions like "What is one thing we can improve in our current process?"

3. One-on-One Conversations

Personal Growth: In individual meetings, explore personal goals: "What motivates you the most in your role, and how can we align your tasks with your motivations?"

Support and Guidance: Offer support by asking, "What challenges are you currently facing, and how can I assist you in overcoming them?"

Case Study: Transformative Questioning in Action

Consider a scenario where a manager, faced with a stagnating project, decides to revitalize the team's approach through strategic questioning. By conducting a series of focused one-on-one and group sessions, the manager asks questions designed to uncover hidden barriers and inspire creative solutions.

Initial Inquiry: "What do you think is the biggest obstacle to our project's success?"

Team Response: Team members identify various technical and communication issues.

Follow-Up: "Can you describe a time when we successfully overcame similar challenges? What did we do differently then?"

Team Reflection: The team recalls past successes and identifies key strategies that can be reapplied.

Action-Oriented: "What immediate steps can we take to address the obstacles you've mentioned?"

Team Collaboration: The team brainstorms actionable steps and assigns responsibilities.

As a result, the project sees renewed energy and progress, driven by the team's collective insights and commitment.

The Broader Implications of Effective Questioning

Effective questioning has implications beyond immediate problem-solving. It fosters a culture of curiosity, continuous learning, and open communication. Organizations prioritizing powerful questioning at all levels are more likely to innovate and adapt to a rapidly changing business environment.

1. Cultivating a Learning Organization

Continuous Improvement: A questioning culture promotes continuous improvement and adaptability.

Knowledge Sharing: Open questions encourage sharing knowledge and best practices across the organization.

2. Enhancing Leadership Effectiveness

Empowered Teams: Leaders who ask the right questions empower their teams to take ownership of their work and contribute meaningfully to organizational goals.

Informed Decision-Making: By seeking diverse perspectives through questioning, leaders make more informed and effective decisions.

Practical Applications: Tools and Techniques

To implement these principles, managers can utilize various tools and techniques:

1. Questioning Frameworks: Develop frameworks for questions (e.g., exploratory, reflective, action-oriented) to guide conversations.
2. Training Programs: Offer training sessions on effective questioning and active listening skills.
3. Feedback Mechanisms: Implement regular feedback loops where team members can ask and answer questions related to ongoing projects.

Conclusion

The power of asking the right questions cannot be overstated. It is a fundamental skill that drives engagement, fosters innovation and enhances leadership effectiveness. By mastering the art of questioning, managers can unlock the full potential of their teams and achieve outstanding results.

As we explore effective management practices in subsequent chapters, remember that the journey to getting things done starts with a simple yet powerful question. Embrace the techniques and strategies this chapter discusses to create a dynamic and thriving organization.

This concludes the fourth chapter of "Managed (To Get It Done)." The following chapters will build on these foundational concepts, providing deeper insights and practical guidance for managers striving to create a dynamic and successful work environment.

Chapter 5
Mastering Communication and Team-Building

Introduction: The Pillars of Effective Management

Linda A. Hill, a renowned expert in leadership and management, emphasizes that mastering communication and team-building is crucial for any manager aiming to foster a high-performing and cohesive team. This chapter delves into the strategies and practices underpinning effective communication and the principles that drive successful team-building. By focusing on these critical areas, managers can create an environment where collaboration thrives, and individuals are empowered to contribute their best.

The Fundamentals of Effective Communication

1.   Understanding Communication Styles

Diverse Styles: Recognize that team members have different communication styles. Some may be direct and assertive, while others might be more reserved and reflective.

Adaptability: Effective managers adapt their communication style to meet the needs of their team members, ensuring clarity and mutual understanding.

2. Active Listening
Engagement: Active listening involves fully engaging with the speaker, showing genuine interest in their message, and providing feedback.

Empathy: Demonstrating empathy by acknowledging the speaker's emotions and perspectives fosters trust and openness.

3. Clarity and Conciseness
Clear Messages: Ensure your messages are clear, concise, and jargon-free. This minimizes misunderstandings and keeps communication efficient.

Purposeful Communication: Every communication should have a clear purpose, whether to inform, request, or provide feedback.

Building a Collaborative Team Culture
1. Defining Team Roles and Responsibilities
Clarity in Roles: Clearly define each team member's role and responsibilities to avoid overlap and confusion.

Aligning with Strengths: Assign roles based on individual strengths and skills to maximize team effectiveness.

2. Creating a Shared Vision
Common Goals: Develop and communicate a shared vision that aligns with the team's goals and objectives.

Involvement: Involve team members in goal-setting to ensure buy-in and commitment.

3. Fostering Trust and Psychological Safety
Trust Building: Build trust through consistent actions, transparency, and reliability.

Psychological Safety: Create an environment where team members feel safe to express their ideas, take risks, and make mistakes without fear of retribution.

Effective Team Communication Strategies

1.   Regular Team Meetings

Structured Agendas: Hold regular team meetings with structured agendas to keep discussions focused and productive.

Open Forums: Provide opportunities for open discussions where team members can voice concerns, share ideas, and provide feedback.

2.   Collaborative Tools and Technologies

Technology Utilization: Utilize collaborative tools and technologies such as project management software, instant messaging, and video conferencing to facilitate seamless communication.

Consistency: Ensure all team members are familiar with and use the chosen communication tools consistently.

3.   Feedback Mechanisms

Constructive Feedback: Implement regular feedback mechanisms that provide constructive and actionable feedback.

Two-Way Feedback: Encourage two-way feedback, where team members can also provide feedback to managers, fostering a culture of continuous improvement.

Case Study: Transforming a Team through Communication

Consider a scenario where a manager takes over a team plagued by poor communication and low morale. The manager transforms the team dynamics by implementing effective communication strategies and focusing on team-building.

Initial Assessment: The manager conducts one-on-one meetings with each team member to understand their concerns and perspectives.

Findings: Team members feel their ideas need to be heard, and there needs to be more clarity in roles.

Action Plan: The manager develops a comprehensive communication and team-building plan.

Regular Meetings: Introduces regular team meetings with clear agendas and open forums for discussion.

Role Clarity: Clearly defines roles and responsibilities, aligning them with individual strengths.

Trust Building: Takes consistent actions to build trust, such as being transparent about decisions and providing reliable support.

Outcome: Over time, the team becomes more cohesive, communication improves, and overall performance increases.

The Broader Implications of Communication and Team-Building

Effective communication and team-building extend beyond immediate team dynamics. They contribute to a positive organizational culture, enhanced employee engagement, and overall organizational success.

1. Cultural Transformation

Inclusive Culture: Foster an inclusive culture where diverse perspectives are valued and everyone feels heard.

Engagement: High levels of communication and team-building lead to increased employee engagement and satisfaction.

2. Organizational Performance

Efficiency: Clear communication and defined roles improve efficiency and reduce the risk of errors.

Innovation: A collaborative team environment fosters innovation and creative problem-solving.

Practical Applications: Tools and Techniques

To implement these principles, managers can utilize various tools and techniques:

1.   Communication Training: Offer programs on practical communication skills, including active listening and empathetic communication.
2.   Team-Building Activities: Organize regular team-building activities that strengthen relationships and foster a sense of community.
3.   Feedback Systems: Implement systems that facilitate regular and constructive feedback exchanges between managers and team members.

Conclusion

Mastering communication and team-building is a cornerstone of effective management. By focusing on these areas, managers can create a dynamic and thriving team environment where collaboration and trust are paramount. The principles and strategies discussed in this chapter provide a foundation for building strong, cohesive teams capable of achieving outstanding results.

As we move forward in "Managed (To Get It Done)," the following chapters will continue to explore essential management practices, providing deeper insights and practical guidance for managers committed to fostering high-performing teams and driving organizational success.

This concludes the fifth chapter of "Managed (To Get It Done)." The following chapters will build on these foundational concepts, offering further insights and actionable strategies for effective management and leadership.

Chapter 6
Leading People and Managing Processes

Introduction: The Dual Imperatives of Leadership and Management

In today's dynamic business environment, managers must balance the dual imperatives of leading people and managing processes. Kory Kogon, Suzette Blakemore, and James Wood emphasize that successful leaders blend the art of people leadership with the science of process management. This chapter explores harmonizing these critical aspects to drive organizational performance and achieve outstanding results.

Section 1: The Principles of Effective Leadership
1.   Vision and Direction
Articulating a Clear Vision: A compelling vision provides direction and inspires team members to align their efforts with organizational goals.

Communicating the Vision: Effective leaders consistently communicate the vision, ensuring that every team member understands their role in achieving it.

2.   Empowering and Developing People

Delegation and Trust: Empower team members by delegating responsibilities and trusting them to execute tasks effectively.

Coaching and Mentorship: Invest in developing team members through coaching and mentorship, helping them grow their skills and capabilities.

3. Emotional Intelligence

Self-Awareness and Self-Regulation: Leaders with high emotional intelligence know their emotions and can regulate them to maintain composure and effectiveness.

Empathy and Social Skills: Understanding and addressing the emotions of others fosters solid relationships and a positive team environment.

Section 2: Managing Processes for Efficiency and Effectiveness

1. Process Optimization

Identifying Key Processes: Focus on critical processes that have the most significant impact on organizational performance.

Streamlining and Standardizing: Simplify processes to eliminate redundancies and standardize them to ensure consistency and efficiency.

2. Continuous Improvement

Lean and Six Sigma: Adopt methodologies like Lean and Six Sigma to drive continuous improvement and eliminate waste.

Feedback Loops: Implement feedback mechanisms to gather input from team members and stakeholders, using it to refine processes continuously.

3. Performance Metrics

Setting Clear Metrics: Define measurable performance metrics that align with organizational goals.

Monitoring and Reporting: Regularly monitor performance against these metrics and report progress to keep the team focused and accountable.

Section 3: Integrating Leadership and Management

1. Aligning People and Processes

Synergy Between Roles and Processes: Ensure that the roles and responsibilities of team members are aligned with optimized processes.

Cross-Functional Collaboration: Foster collaboration across functions to enhance process efficiency and innovation.

2. Balancing Short-Term and Long-Term Goals

Operational Excellence: Focus on achieving short-term operational goals through efficient process management.

Strategic Leadership: Simultaneously, maintain a long-term strategic focus, guiding the team toward future objectives.

3. Cultural Alignment

Creating a High-Performance Culture: Develop a culture that values effective leadership and efficient process management.

Continuous Learning and Adaptability: Encourage a continuous learning and adaptability culture, where team members are open to change and innovation.

Case Study: Transformative Leadership and Process Management

Consider the case of a mid-sized company struggling with inefficiencies and low employee morale. A new manager, well-versed in the principles outlined by Kory Kogon, Suzette Blakemore, and James Wood, takes the helm.

Initial Assessment: The manager thoroughly assesses the team's capabilities and existing processes.

Findings: The team needs a clear vision, and processes need to be more efficient and updated.

Vision and Empowerment: The manager articulates a clear vision for the company, focusing on innovation and customer satisfaction.

Action Plan: The manager empowers team members by delegating responsibilities and providing the necessary support and training.

Process Optimization: The manager introduces Lean methodologies to streamline critical processes.

Continuous Improvement: Feedback loops are implemented to gather insights and improve processes.

Outcome: Over time, the company experiences improved efficiency, higher employee engagement, and better overall performance.

Practical Applications: Tools and Techniques

To implement these principles effectively, managers can utilize a variety of tools and techniques:

1. **Leadership Development Programs:**
Invest in programs that develop leadership skills, such as emotional intelligence and strategic visioning.

2. **Process Improvement Workshops:**
Conduct workshops focused on process improvement methodologies like Lean and Six Sigma.

3. **Performance Management Systems:**
Implement systems that track performance metrics and provide real-time feedback to team members.

Conclusion

Leading people and managing processes are not mutually exclusive tasks; they are interdependent and critical for organizational success. By integrating effective leadership with efficient process management, managers can create an environment where individuals thrive and optimize processes for maximum performance. The principles and strategies discussed in this chapter provide a roadmap for achieving this balance, leading to sustained success and continuous improvement.

As we progress in "Managed (To Get It Done)," the subsequent chapters will continue to build on these foundational concepts, offering further insights and practical guidance for effective management and leadership.

This concludes the sixth chapter of "Managed (To Get It Done)." The following chapters will delve deeper into the intricacies of managing people and processes, providing actionable strategies and real-world examples to guide managers on their journey toward excellence.

Chapter 7
Handling Difficult Conversations with Tact

Introduction: The Art of Tactful Communication

Difficult conversations are an inevitable part of managing people. Whether addressing performance issues, resolving conflicts, or delivering bad news, these conversations require empathy, clarity, and assertiveness. Paul Falcone, a renowned expert in HR and leadership, provides a wealth of insights into handling these situations tactfully and professionally. This chapter will explore strategies to navigate difficult conversations effectively, ensuring they lead to positive outcomes and strengthened relationships.

Section 1: Preparing for the Conversation
1.   Clarity and Purpose

Define the Objective: Clearly understand the purpose of the conversation. Is it to address a performance issue, provide feedback, or resolve a conflict? Having a clear objective helps in structuring the conversation.

Gather Facts: Collect all relevant information and evidence. Avoid relying on hearsay or assumptions, as presenting concrete facts will lend credibility to your discussion.

2.   Emotional Readiness

Self-Reflection: Assess your emotional state. Entering a difficult conversation with a calm and composed mindset is crucial.

Empathy and Understanding: Try to understand the other person's perspective. Consider their feelings and potential reactions.

3.   Environment and Timing

Choose an Appropriate Setting: Select a private, neutral location where the conversation can occur without interruptions.

Timing is Key: Ensure the timing is suitable for both parties. Avoid initiating difficult conversations during high-stress periods or in public settings.

Section 2: Structuring the Conversation
1.   Opening the Dialogue

Establish a Positive Tone: Start the conversation on a positive note. Acknowledge the person's contributions and express your intention to resolve the issue constructively.

State the Purpose Clearly: Clearly explain the reason for the conversation. Be direct yet compassionate.

2.   Presenting the Issue

Focus on Behavior, Not Personality: Address specific behaviors or actions rather than making it about the person's character. This approach reduces defensiveness and keeps the conversation objective.

Use "I" Statements: Frame your observations using "I" statements to express how the behavior impacts you or the team. For example, "I noticed that..." or "I feel that..."

3.   Active Listening

Encourage Open Dialogue: Allow the other person to share their perspective without interruption. Active listening demonstrates respect and helps in understanding their viewpoint.

Reflect and Clarify: Paraphrase what the other person says to ensure understanding. Ask clarifying questions if needed.

Section 3: Finding Common Ground and Solutions

1.   Collaborative Problem-Solving

Identify Mutual Goals: Focus on shared objectives and mutual interests. This alignment fosters cooperation and a sense of shared purpose.

Brainstorm Solutions Together: Involve the other person in generating solutions. This collaborative approach increases buy-in and commitment to the resolution.

2.   Setting Expectations

Define Clear Action Steps: Outline specific actions that need to be taken by both parties. Ensure these steps are realistic and measurable.

Establish a Timeline: Set a timeline for follow-up and review. This helps monitor progress and make necessary adjustments.

3.   Closing the Conversation

Summarize Key Points: Recap the main points discussed and the agreed-upon action steps.

Express Confidence: End the conversation positively, expressing confidence in the other person's ability to improve and succeed.

Case Study: Navigating a Performance Issue

Consider the case of a manager, Sarah, who needs to address a performance issue with one of her team members, John. John needs to meet deadlines, affecting the team's overall productivity consistently.

Preparation: Sarah gathers specific examples of missed deadlines and their impact on the team. She reflects on her emotions and prepares to approach the conversation with empathy and a clear objective.

Environment: Sarah schedules a private meeting with John in a neutral setting.

Opening the Dialogue: Sarah starts by acknowledging John's hard work and contributions to the team.

Presenting the Issue: She clearly states the purpose of the conversation and presents the specific instances of missed deadlines using "I" statements to express her concerns.

Active Listening: John explains his side, mentioning personal challenges he has been facing. Sarah listens attentively and reflects on his points.

Finding Common Ground: They identify mutual goals—ensuring the team meets its deadlines and supporting John in managing his workload.

Collaborative Problem-Solving: They brainstorm potential solutions, such as adjusting John's workload and providing additional support.

Setting Expectations: They define clear action steps and set a timeline for follow-up.

Closing the Conversation: Sarah summarizes the key points and action steps, expressing confidence in John's ability to improve.

Practical Applications: Tools and Techniques

To handle difficult conversations effectively, managers can utilize various tools and techniques:

1.   Role-Playing: Practice difficult conversations through role-playing exercises. This helps anticipate potential responses and refine your approach.
2.   Feedback Models: Use structured feedback models like the SBI (Situation-Behavior-Impact) model to provide clear and objective feedback.
3.   Conflict Resolution Training: Invest in training programs focused on conflict resolution and practical communication skills.

Conclusion

Handling difficult conversations with tact is a vital skill for managers. Managers can successfully navigate these challenging interactions by preparing thoroughly, structuring the conversation effectively, and focusing on collaborative solutions. Paul Falcone's principles offer a practical roadmap for conducting these conversations with empathy, clarity, and professionalism.

As we conclude this chapter, remember that when handled well, difficult conversations can lead to significant growth and improvement for both individuals and the organization. The next chapter will continue to build on these concepts, offering further insights and strategies for effective management.

Conclusion

As we bring this journey to a close, let us reflect on the seven powerful principles we have explored. These principles, drawn from the wisdom of leading experts in management and leadership, provide a robust framework for effectively managing people and driving exceptional results.

Chapter 1: Maximizing Human Potential

The key to maximizing human potential lies in understanding and leveraging individual strengths. As Clifton and Harter highlight in their comprehensive research on workplace management, recognizing the unique abilities of each team member and aligning their roles to these strengths is crucial for long-term success.[1]

Chapter 2: Building Trust and Motivating Beyond Authority

Trust is the foundation of effective management. According to The Harvard Business Review Manager's Handbook, building trust requires consistency, integrity, and a genuine concern for team members' well-being.[2] By fostering a

---

[1] Jim Clifton and Jim Harter, It is the Manager: Gallup Finds the Quality of Managers and Team Leaders Is the Single Biggest Factor in Your Organization's Long-Term Success.

[2] The Harvard Business Review, The Harvard Business Review Manager's Handbook: The 17 Skills Leaders Need to Stand Out.

culture of trust, managers can inspire their teams to exceed expectations and achieve extraordinary results.

Chapter 3: Investing in Personal Development
Investing in personal development is essential for both individual and organizational growth. Miller, Davis, and Roos Olsson emphasize the importance of continuous learning and professional development as key drivers of employee engagement and retention.[3] Providing opportunities for skill enhancement and career progression can significantly boost morale and productivity.

Chapter 4: The Power of Asking the Right Questions
Ryan Hawk underscores the transformative power of asking the right questions in fostering a culture of curiosity and continuous improvement.[4] By encouraging open dialogue and critical thinking, managers can uncover valuable insights and drive innovation within their teams.

Chapter 5: Mastering Communication and Team-Building
Effective communication and team-building are fundamental to successful management. Linda A. Hill discusses how clear communication and a strong team dynamic can enhance collaboration, resolve conflicts, and achieve common goals.[5] Developing these skills is vital for

---

[3] Scott Jeffrey Miller, Todd Davis, and Victoria Roos Olsson, Everyone Deserves a Great Manager: The 6 Critical Practices for Leading a Team.

[4] Ryan Hawk, Welcome to Management: How to Grow From Top Performer to Excellent Leader.

[5] Linda A. Hill, Becoming a Manager: How New Managers Master the Challenges of Leadership.

any manager looking to create a cohesive and high-performing team.

Chapter 6: Leading People and Managing Processes

Kory Kogon, Suzette Blakemore, and James Wood highlight the importance of balancing people management with process optimization.[6] Effective leaders understand how to manage their team's dynamics while streamlining processes to enhance efficiency and productivity.

Chapter 7: Handling Difficult Conversations with Tact

Paul Falcone provides valuable strategies for handling difficult conversations with tact and sensitivity.[7] Addressing issues directly but compassionately can prevent misunderstandings and foster a positive work environment.

Bringing It All Together

Each chapter has provided valuable insights and practical strategies for managing people effectively. As you move forward, remember that the essence of excellent management lies in balancing empathy with assertiveness, vision with pragmatism, and authority with trust.

The principles outlined in this book are not just theoretical concepts but actionable strategies that can transform your approach to management. These principles will help you build a resilient, motivated, and high-performing team.

---

[6] Kory Kogon, Suzette Blakemore, and James Wood, Project Management for the Unofficial Project Manager: A FranklinCovey Title.

[7] Paul Falcone, 75 Ways for Managers to Hire, Develop, and Keep Great Employees.

A Call to Action

Management is an ongoing journey of learning, adaptation, and growth. As you apply these principles, remain open to feedback and committed to continuous improvement. Encourage your team to share their ideas, celebrate successes, and learn from challenges together.

Remember, great managers are not born; they are made through dedication, experience, and a genuine desire to bring out the best in their people. You have the tools, insights, and strategies at your disposal to become the leader your team needs.

Final Thoughts

As you close this book, take a moment to reflect on your journey as a manager. Consider the impact you want on your team and the legacy you wish to leave. Use the principles and strategies outlined in these chapters as your guide to managing people and truly inspiring and empowering them.

Thank you for embarking on this journey with me. Now, go forth and manage to get It done.

References

Clifton, J., and Harter, J. (2019). *It is the manager: Gallup finds the quality of managers and team leaders is the single biggest factor in your organization's long-term success.* Gallup Press.

Falcone, P. (2016). *75 ways for managers to hire, develop, and keep great employees.* Amacom.

Hawk, R. (2020). *Welcome to management: How to grow from top performer to excellent leader.* McGraw-Hill Education.

Hill, L. A. (2003). *Becoming a manager: How new managers master the challenges of leadership.* Harvard Business Review Press.

Kogon, K., Blakemore, S., and Wood, J. (2015). *Project management for the unofficial project manager: A FranklinCovey title.* BenBella Books.

Miller, S. J., Davis, T., and Olsson, V. R. (2019). *Everyone deserves a great manager: The 6 critical practices for leading a team.* Simon & Schuster.

The Harvard Business Review. (2017). *The Harvard Business Review manager's handbook: The 17 skills leaders need to stand out.* Harvard Business Review Press.

www.ingramcontent.com/pod-product-compliance
Lightning Source LLC
Chambersburg PA
CBHW070421240526
45472CB00019B/540